PLATE 1. Wall Decorations

DECORATIONS
FOR WALLS & PANELS
Early Twentieth-Century Design & Pattern

KARL LÜTH

DOVER PUBLICATIONS, INC.
Mineola, New York

KARL LÜTH · KIEL

Stencil Factory
Artisanal Studio

Offering the services of my decorative painting workshop for the preparation of

All Kinds of Sketches and Designs

in every style for ceilings, walls, stairwells, kitchens, halls, etc. Upon request will also send competent, trained workers to complete decorative projects for a moderate fee.

All stencils are very carefully cut by hand, produced on the best stencil paper, and impregnated once with good oil. For all motifs, the stencils are first cut, then assembled in the layout shown here, and then reduced. Thus, these samples constitute a faithful rendering at reduced scale of the stencils offered for sale. Unless otherwise indicated, stencils are without breaks; nothing is painted in by hand. Therefore, everything can be stenciled just as shown in the book. — Individual friezes, etc., can also be derived from the overall designs.

All of the examples in the book are shown at a scale of 1 : 10.

The sale of my patterns is subject to payment on delivery.

Bibliographical Note

This Dover edition, first published in 2018, is an unabridged republication of *Moderne Wand und Decken Dekoration*, originally published by Krey and Sommerlad, Niedersedutz-Dresden, c.1900. For this edition, the Introduction and the captions have been translated into English.

Library of Congress Cataloging-in-Publication Data

Names: Karl Lüth (Firm), author.
Title: Decorations for walls and panels : early twentieth-century design and pattern / Karl Lüth .
Other titles: Moderne Wand und Decken Dekoration. English
Description: Mineola, New York : Dover Publications, Inc., 2018. | "This Dover edition, first published in 2018, is an unabridged republication of Moderne Wand und Decken Dekoration, originally published by Krey and Sommerlad, Niedersedutz-Dresden, c.1900. For this edition, the Introduction and the captions have been translated into English."
Identifiers: LCCN 2017049762| ISBN 9780486820958 | ISBN 0486820955
Subjects: LCSH: Stencil work—Themes, motives. | Interior walls—Decoration. Ceilings—Decoration.
Classification: LCC NK8669 .K37 2018 | DDC 745.7/3—dc23
LC record available at https://lccn.loc.gov/2017049762

Manufactured in the United States by LSC Communications
82095501   2018
www.doverpublications.com

Plate 2. Wall Decorations

Plate 3. Cover Decorations

PLATE 4. Wall Decorations

Plate 5. Wall Decorations

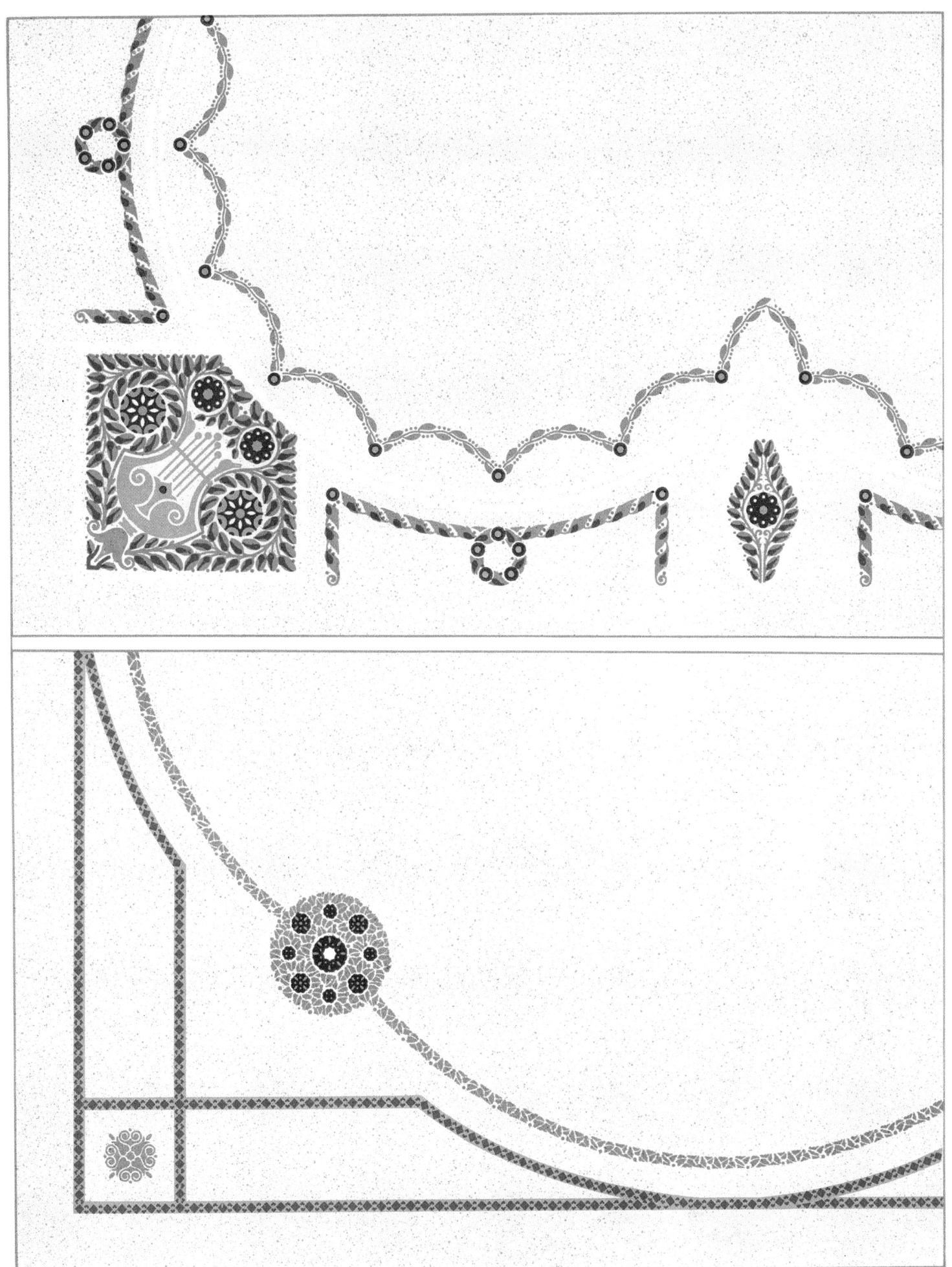

PLATE 6. Cover Decorations for Plates 4 and 5

PLATE 7. Ceiling and Wall Decorations

PLATE 8. Ceiling and Wall Decorations

PLATE 9. Wall Decorations

PLATE 10. Butcher Shop Decoration

PLATE 11. Room Decoration

PLATE 12. Ceiling and Wall Decorations

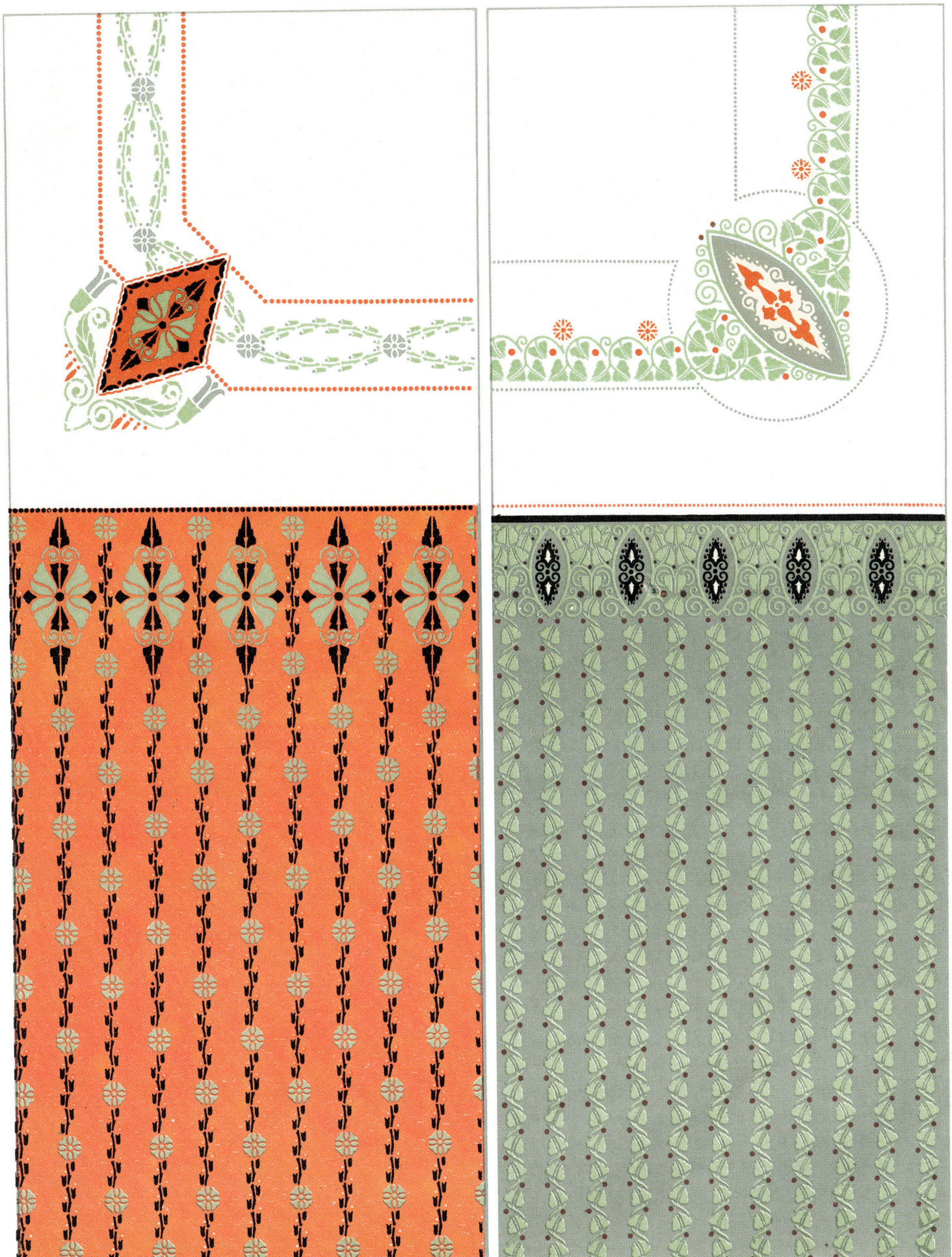

PLATE 13. Ceiling and Wall Decorations

PLATE 14. Ceiling and Wall Decorations

PLATE 15. Ceiling and Wall Decorations

PLATE 16. Ceiling and Wall Decorations

PLATE 17. Ceiling and Wall Decorations

PLATE 18. Bakery and Cake Decoration

PLATE 19. Study Decoration

PLATE 20. Decoration for Rooms and Bowls

PLATE 21. Wall Decorations

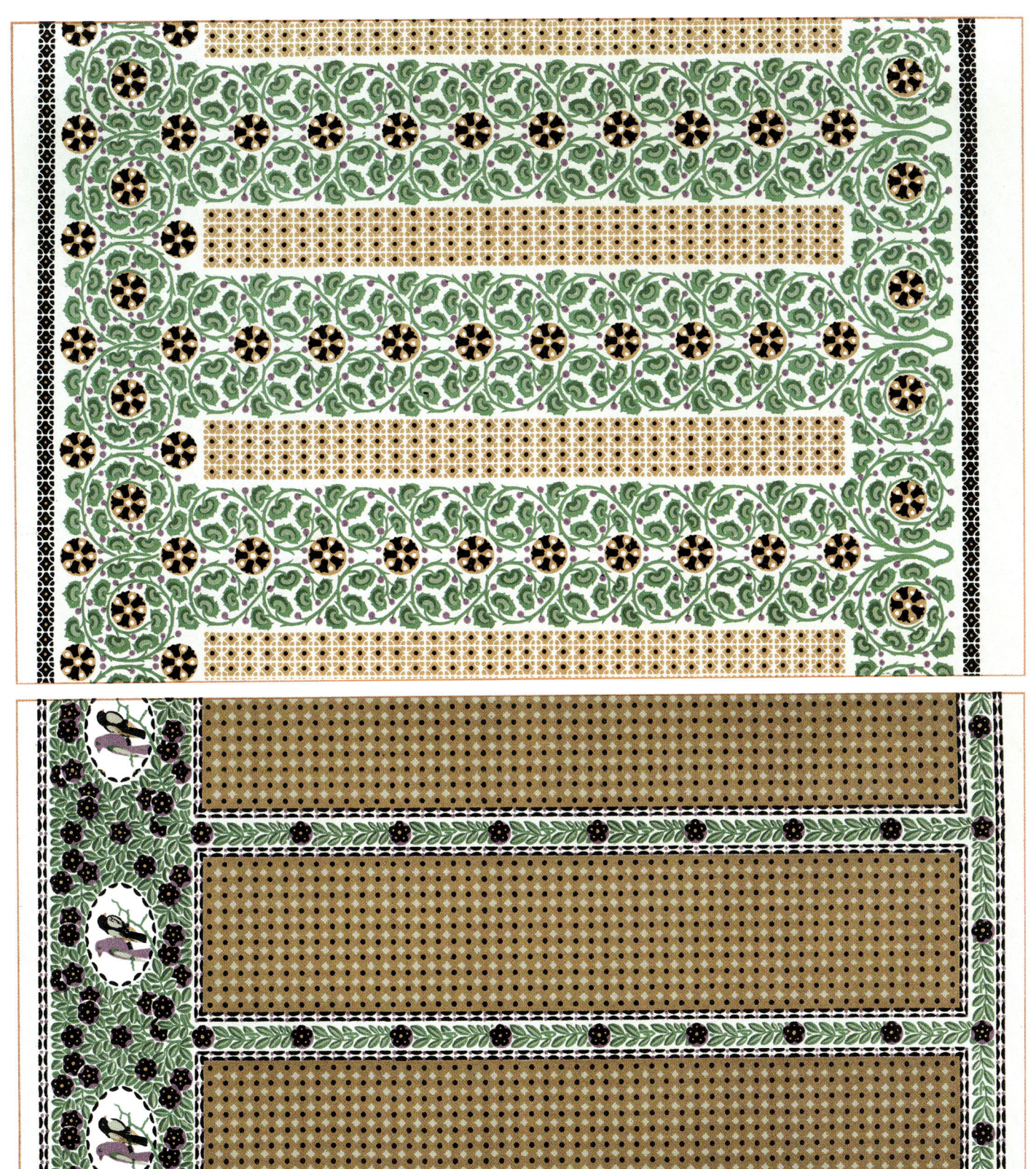

PLATE 22. Wall Decorations

Plate 23 Wall Decorations

PLATE 24. Wall Decorations

Plate 25. Wall Decorations

PLATE 26. Wall Decorations

PLATE 27. Wall Decorations

PLATE 28. Floral Friezes

PLATE 29. Cover Decorations

PLATE 30. Cover Decorations

PLATE 31. Relevant Corners and in the Middle

PLATE 32. Relevant Corners and Rosette

PLATE 33. Various Decorations and Fillings

PLATE 34. Staircase Decoration

PLATE 35. Staircase Decoration

PLATE 36. Staircase Decoration

PLATE 37. Staircase Decoration

PLATE 38. Staircase Decoration

PLATE 39. Staircase Decoration

PLATE 40. Staircase Decoration

PLATE 41. Staircase Decoration

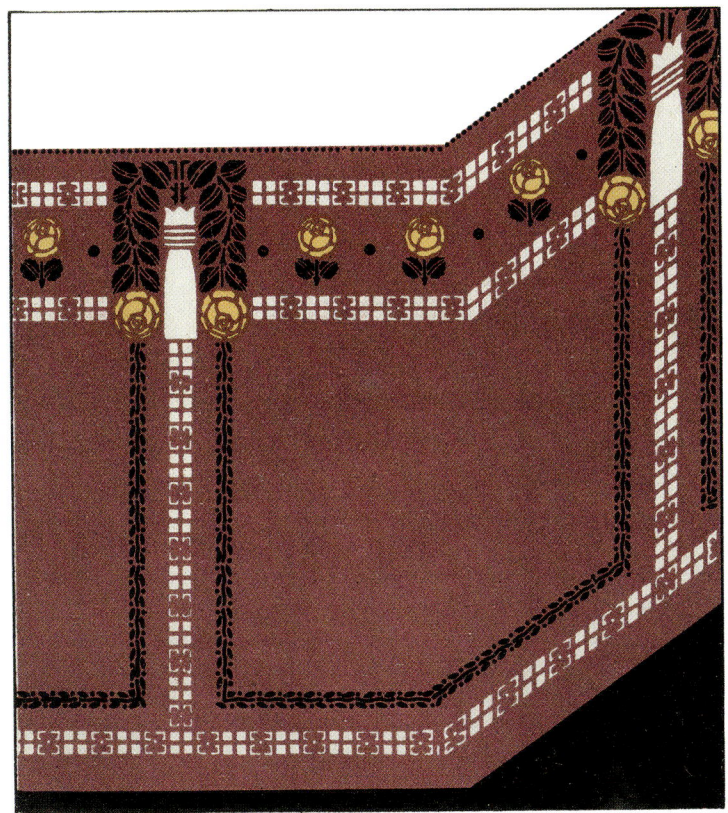

PLATE 42. Staircase Decoration

Plate 43. Staircase Frieze

PLATE 44. Staircase Frieze

Plate 45. Friezes

PLATE 46. Borders and Multi-Layered Friezes

PLATE 47. Wall Decorations

PLATE 48. Friezes

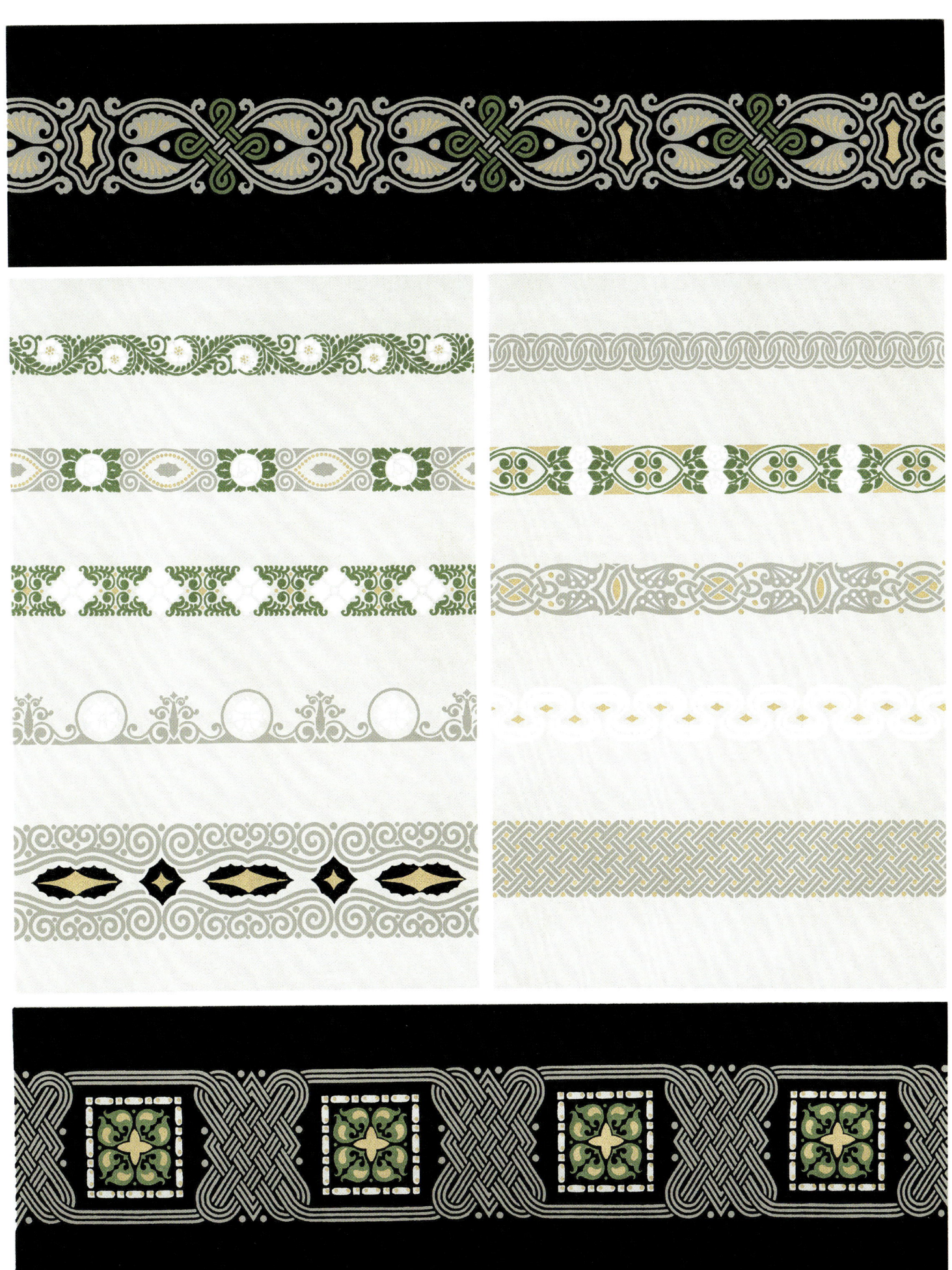

PLATE 49. Friezes

PLATE 50. Borders and Friezes

PLATE 51. Friezes and Borders

PLATE 52. Borders and Friezes

Plate 53. Friezes and Borders

PLATE 54. Friezes and Borders

PLATE 55. Kitchen Friezes and Kitchen Cabinet Ornaments

PLATE 56. Wall Patterns and Borders

PLATE 57. Wall Patterns

PLATE 58. Wall Decorations

PLATE 59. Wall Patterns

PLATE 60. Wall Patterns

PLATE 61. Wall Patterns

PLATE 62. Wall Patterns

PLATE 63. Kitchen Patterns